VISION BOARD

This journal belongs to: ____________________________

VIVIAN TENORIO

VISION BOARD

a journal

BY VIVIAN TENORIO

JAV PUBLISHING

Printed in the United Stated of America

www.viviantenorio.com

ISBN-10: 0615665756
ISBN-13: 978-0615665757

VISION BOARD

Tools & Tips

⌘ Play the picture in your mind - focus on the end result.

⌘ Feel the joy - feel the happiness :o)

⌘ Gratitude will bring more into our lives immediately.

⌘ Learn to become still .. and take your attention away from what you don't want, and place your attention on what you wish to experience.

⌘ Review your goals & desires daily and get into the feeling state of already having acquired these wants.

When you have an inspired thought, you must trust it and act on it.

VISION BOARD - STEPS

Step 1: Ask

Identify and be clear about what you want & desire.

Illustrate your desire and goal with pictures, words, drawings & phrases

Step 2: Allow

Expect that the Universe/God/Spirit will answer. Allow and be grateful AS IF you have already received what you want.

Step 3: Receive

Be grateful and notice even the smallest evidence of the law of attraction. The more you are grateful and paying attention, the faster your desires and goals will manifests.

Step 1: Ask

Identify and be clear about what you want & desire.

Desired by : ____________

____

____

"I ask the universe for my desires."

Step 2: Allow

Expect that the Universe/God/Spirit will answer. Allow and be grateful AS IF you have already received what you want.

IT'S IMPORTANT TO FEEL GOOD ((((((**GOOD**))))))

Remember: thoughts = creation. If these thoughts are attached to powerful emotions (good or bad) that speeds up the creation of your desires.

VISUALIZE!!! *See it, feel it! This is where action begins*

Step 3: Receive

Be grateful and notice even the smallest evidence of the law of attraction. The more you are grateful and paying attention, the faster your desires and goals will manifests.

Start by using this sentence for all that you receive: "I'm so happy and grateful now that....

____

____

____

____

____

____

____

____

____

Received on: ______________

"I have evidence of my abundance."

Step 1: Ask

Identify and be clear about what you want & desire.

Desired by : ____________

"I ask the universe for my desires."

Step 2: Allow

Expect that the Universe/God/Spirit will answer. Allow and be grateful AS IF you have already received what you want.

IT'S IMPORTANT TO FEEL GOOD ((((((**GOOD**))))))

Remember: thoughts = creation. If these thoughts are attached to powerful emotions (good or bad) that speeds up the creation of your desires.

VISUALIZE!!! *See it, feel it! This is where action begins*

Step 3: Receive

Be grateful and notice even the smallest evidence of the law of attraction. The more you are grateful and paying attention, the faster your desires and goals will manifests.

Start by using this sentence for all that you receive: "I'm so happy and grateful now that....

____

____

____

____

____

____

____

____

____

Received on: ____________

"I have evidence of my abundance."

Step 1: Ask

Identify and be clear about what you want & desire.

Desired by : ____________

"I ask the universe for my desires."

Step 2: Allow

Expect that the Universe/God/Spirit will answer. Allow and be grateful AS IF you have already received what you want.

IT'S IMPORTANT TO FEEL GOOD ((((((**GOOD**))))))

Remember: thoughts = creation. If these thoughts are attached to powerful emotions (good or bad) that speeds up the creation of your desires.

VISUALIZE!!! *See it, feel it! This is where action begins*

Step 3: Receive

Be grateful and notice even the smallest evidence of the law of attraction. The more you are grateful and paying attention, the faster your desires and goals will manifests.

Start by using this sentence for all that you receive: "I'm so happy and grateful now that....

____

____

____

____

____

____

____

____

____

Received on: ______________

"I have evidence of my abundance."

Step 1: Ask

Identify and be clear about what you want & desire.

Desired by : ____________

"I ask the universe for my desires."

Step 2: Allow

Expect that the Universe/God/Spirit will answer. Allow and be grateful AS IF you have already received what you want.

IT'S IMPORTANT TO FEEL GOOD ((((((**GOOD**))))))

Remember: thoughts = creation. If these thoughts are attached to powerful emotions (good or bad) that speeds up the creation of your desires.

VISUALIZE!!! *See it, feel it! This is where action begins*

Step 3: Receive

Be grateful and notice even the smallest evidence of the law of attraction. The more you are grateful and paying attention, the faster your desires and goals will manifests.

Start by using this sentence for all that you receive: "I'm so happy and grateful now that....

____

____

____

____

____

____

____

____

____

Received on: ______________

"I have evidence of my abundance."

Step 1: Ask

Identify and be clear about what you want & desire.

Desired by: ____________

"I ask the universe for my desires."

Step 2: Allow

Expect that the Universe/God/Spirit will answer. Allow and be grateful AS IF you have already received what you want.

IT'S IMPORTANT TO FEEL GOOD ((((((**GOOD**))))))

Remember: thoughts = creation. If these thoughts are attached to powerful emotions (good or bad) that speeds up the creation of your desires.

VISUALIZE!!! *See it, feel it! This is where action begins*

Step 3: Receive

Be grateful and notice even the smallest evidence of the law of attraction. The more you are grateful and paying attention, the faster your desires and goals will manifests.

Start by using this sentence for all that you receive: "I'm so happy and grateful now that....

___

___

___

___

___

___

___

___

___

Received on: ______________

"I have evidence of my abundance."

Step 1: Ask

Identify and be clear about what you want & desire.

Desired by : ____________

"I ask the universe for my desires."

Step 2: Allow

Expect that the Universe/God/Spirit will answer. Allow and be grateful AS IF you have already received what you want.

IT'S IMPORTANT TO FEEL GOOD ((((((**GOOD**))))))

Remember: thoughts = creation. If these thoughts are attached to powerful emotions (good or bad) that speeds up the creation of your desires.

VISUALIZE!!! *See it, feel it! This is where action begins*

Step 3: Receive

Be grateful and notice even the smallest evidence of the law of attraction. The more you are grateful and paying attention, the faster your desires and goals will manifests.

Start by using this sentence for all that you receive: "I'm so happy and grateful now that....

____

____

____

____

____

____

____

____

____

Received on: ____________

"I have evidence of my abundance."

Step 1: Ask

Identify and be clear about what you want & desire.

Desired by : ____________

____

____

"I ask the universe for my desires."

Step 2: Allow

Expect that the Universe/God/Spirit will answer. Allow and be grateful AS IF you have already received what you want.

IT'S IMPORTANT TO FEEL GOOD ((((((**GOOD**))))))

Remember: thoughts = creation. If these thoughts are attached to powerful emotions (good or bad) that speeds up the creation of your desires.

VISUALIZE!!! *See it, feel it! This is where action begins*

Step 3: Receive

Be grateful and notice even the smallest evidence of the law of attraction. The more you are grateful and paying attention, the faster your desires and goals will manifests.

Start by using this sentence for all that you receive: "I'm so happy and grateful now that....

Received on: ______________

"I have evidence of my abundance."

Step 1: Ask

Identify and be clear about what you want & desire.

Desired by : ____________

___

___

"I ask the universe for my desires."

Step 2: Allow

Expect that the Universe/God/Spirit will answer. Allow and be grateful AS IF you have already received what you want.

IT'S IMPORTANT TO FEEL GOOD ((((((**GOOD**))))))

Remember: thoughts = creation. If these thoughts are attached to powerful emotions (good or bad) that speeds up the creation of your desires.

VISUALIZE!!! *See it, feel it! This is where action begins*

Step 3: Receive

Be grateful and notice even the smallest evidence of the law of attraction. The more you are grateful and paying attention, the faster your desires and goals will manifests.

Start by using this sentence for all that you receive: "I'm so happy and grateful now that....

____

____

____

____

____

____

____

____

____

Received on: ________________

"I have evidence of my abundance."

Step 1: Ask

Identify and be clear about what you want & desire.

Desired by : ___________

"I ask the universe for my desires."

Step 2: Allow

Expect that the Universe/God/Spirit will answer. Allow and be grateful AS IF you have already received what you want.

IT'S IMPORTANT TO FEEL GOOD ((((((**GOOD**))))))

Remember: thoughts = creation. If these thoughts are attached to powerful emotions (good or bad) that speeds up the creation of your desires.

VISUALIZE!!! *See it, feel it! This is where action begins*

Step 3: Receive

Be grateful and notice even the smallest evidence of the law of attraction. The more you are grateful and paying attention, the faster your desires and goals will manifests.

Start by using this sentence for all that you receive: "I'm so happy and grateful now that....

____

____

____

____

____

____

____

____

____

Received on: ______________

"I have evidence of my abundance."

Step 1: Ask

Identify and be clear about what you want & desire.

Desired by : ___________

____

____

"I ask the universe for my desires."

Step 2: Allow

Expect that the Universe/God/Spirit will answer. Allow and be grateful AS IF you have already received what you want.

IT'S IMPORTANT TO FEEL GOOD ((((((**GOOD**))))))

Remember: thoughts = creation. If these thoughts are attached to powerful emotions (good or bad) that speeds up the creation of your desires.

VISUALIZE!!! *See it, feel it! This is where action begins*

Step 3: Receive

Be grateful and notice even the smallest evidence of the law of attraction. The more you are grateful and paying attention, the faster your desires and goals will manifests.

Start by using this sentence for all that you receive: "I'm so happy and grateful now that....

____

____

____

____

____

____

____

____

____

Received on: ____________

"I have evidence of my abundance."

Step 1: Ask

Identify and be clear about what you want & desire.

Desired by : ____________

____

____

"I ask the universe for my desires."

Step 2: Allow

Expect that the Universe/God/Spirit will answer. Allow and be grateful AS IF you have already received what you want.

IT'S IMPORTANT TO FEEL GOOD ((((((**GOOD**))))))

Remember: thoughts = creation. If these thoughts are attached to powerful emotions (good or bad) that speeds up the creation of your desires.

VISUALIZE!!! *See it, feel it! This is where action begins*

Step 3: Receive

Be grateful and notice even the smallest evidence of the law of attraction. The more you are grateful and paying attention, the faster your desires and goals will manifests.

Start by using this sentence for all that you receive: "I'm so happy and grateful now that....

Received on: ______________

"I have evidence of my abundance."

Step 1: Ask

Identify and be clear about what you want & desire.

Desired by : ____________

____

____

"I ask the universe for my desires."

Step 2: Allow

Expect that the Universe/God/Spirit will answer. Allow and be grateful AS IF you have already received what you want.

IT'S IMPORTANT TO FEEL GOOD ((((((**GOOD**))))))

Remember: thoughts = creation. If these thoughts are attached to powerful emotions (good or bad) that speeds up the creation of your desires.

VISUALIZE!!! *See it, feel it! This is where action begins*

Step 3: Receive

Be grateful and notice even the smallest evidence of the law of attraction. The more you are grateful and paying attention, the faster your desires and goals will manifests.

Start by using this sentence for all that you receive: "I'm so happy and grateful now that....

____

____

____

____

____

____

____

____

____

Received on: ______________

"I have evidence of my abundance."

Step 1: Ask

Identify and be clear about what you want & desire.

Desired by : ____________

____

____

"I ask the universe for my desires."

Step 2: Allow

Expect that the Universe/God/Spirit will answer. Allow and be grateful AS IF you have already received what you want.

IT'S IMPORTANT TO FEEL GOOD ((((((**GOOD**))))))

Remember: thoughts = creation. If these thoughts are attached to powerful emotions (good or bad) that speeds up the creation of your desires.

VISUALIZE!!! *See it, feel it! This is where action begins*

Step 3: Receive

Be grateful and notice even the smallest evidence of the law of attraction. The more you are grateful and paying attention, the faster your desires and goals will manifests.

Start by using this sentence for all that you receive: "I'm so happy and grateful now that....

____

____

____

____

____

____

____

____

____

Received on: ______________

"I have evidence of my abundance."

Step 1: Ask

Identify and be clear about what you want & desire.

Desired by : ___________

"I ask the universe for my desires."

Step 2: Allow

Expect that the Universe/God/Spirit will answer. Allow and be grateful AS IF you have already received what you want.

IT'S IMPORTANT TO FEEL GOOD ((((((**GOOD**))))))

Remember: thoughts = creation. If these thoughts are attached to powerful emotions (good or bad) that speeds up the creation of your desires.

VISUALIZE!!! *See it, feel it! This is where action begins*

Step 3: Receive

Be grateful and notice even the smallest evidence of the law of attraction. The more you are grateful and paying attention, the faster your desires and goals will manifests.

Start by using this sentence for all that you receive: "I'm so happy and grateful now that....

____

____

____

____

____

____

____

____

____

Received on: ______________

"I have evidence of my abundance."

Step 1: Ask

Identify and be clear about what you want & desire.

Desired by : ____________

"I ask the universe for my desires."

Step 2: Allow

Expect that the Universe/God/Spirit will answer. Allow and be grateful AS IF you have already received what you want.

IT'S IMPORTANT TO FEEL GOOD ((((((**GOOD**))))))

Remember: thoughts = creation. If these thoughts are attached to powerful emotions (good or bad) that speeds up the creation of your desires.

VISUALIZE!!! *See it, feel it! This is where action begins*

Step 3: Receive

Be grateful and notice even the smallest evidence of the law of attraction. The more you are grateful and paying attention, the faster your desires and goals will manifests.

Start by using this sentence for all that you receive: "I'm so happy and grateful now that....

____

____

____

____

____

____

____

____

____

Received on: ____________

"I have evidence of my abundance."

Step 1: Ask

Identify and be clear about what you want & desire.

Desired by : ____________

____

____

"I ask the universe for my desires."

Step 2: Allow

Expect that the Universe/God/Spirit will answer. Allow and be grateful AS IF you have already received what you want.

IT'S IMPORTANT TO FEEL GOOD ((((((**GOOD**))))))

Remember: thoughts = creation. If these thoughts are attached to powerful emotions (good or bad) that speeds up the creation of your desires.

VISUALIZE!!! *See it, feel it! This is where action begins*

Step 3: Receive

Be grateful and notice even the smallest evidence of the law of attraction. The more you are grateful and paying attention, the faster your desires and goals will manifests.

Start by using this sentence for all that you receive: "I'm so happy and grateful now that....

____

____

____

____

____

____

____

____

____

Received on: ____________

"I have evidence of my abundance."

Step 1: Ask

Identify and be clear about what you want & desire.

Desired by: ____________

____

____

"I ask the universe for my desires."

Step 2: Allow

Expect that the Universe/God/Spirit will answer. Allow and be grateful AS IF you have already received what you want.

IT'S IMPORTANT TO FEEL GOOD ((((((**GOOD**))))))

Remember: thoughts = creation. If these thoughts are attached to powerful emotions (good or bad) that speeds up the creation of your desires.

VISUALIZE!!! *See it, feel it! This is where action begins*

Step 3: Receive

Be grateful and notice even the smallest evidence of the law of attraction. The more you are grateful and paying attention, the faster your desires and goals will manifests.

Start by using this sentence for all that you receive: "I'm so happy and grateful now that....

____

____

____

____

____

____

____

____

____

Received on: ______________

"I have evidence of my abundance."

Step 1: Ask

Identify and be clear about what you want & desire.

Desired by : ____________

"*I ask the universe for my desires.*"

Step 2: Allow

Expect that the Universe/God/Spirit will answer. Allow and be grateful AS IF you have already received what you want.

IT'S IMPORTANT TO FEEL GOOD ((((((**GOOD**))))))

Remember: thoughts = creation. If these thoughts are attached to powerful emotions (good or bad) that speeds up the creation of your desires.

VISUALIZE!!! *See it, feel it! This is where action begins*

Step 3: Receive

Be grateful and notice even the smallest evidence of the law of attraction. The more you are grateful and paying attention, the faster your desires and goals will manifests.

Start by using this sentence for all that you receive: "I'm so happy and grateful now that....

____

____

____

____

____

____

____

____

____

Received on: ______________

"I have evidence of my abundance."

Step 1: Ask

Identify and be clear about what you want & desire.

Desired by : ___________

"I ask the universe for my desires."

Step 2: Allow

Expect that the Universe/God/Spirit will answer. Allow and be grateful AS IF you have already received what you want.

IT'S IMPORTANT TO FEEL GOOD ((((((**GOOD**))))))

Remember: thoughts = creation. If these thoughts are attached to powerful emotions (good or bad) that speeds up the creation of your desires.

VISUALIZE!!! *See it, feel it! This is where action begins*

Step 3: Receive

Be grateful and notice even the smallest evidence of the law of attraction. The more you are grateful and paying attention, the faster your desires and goals will manifests.

Start by using this sentence for all that you receive: "I'm so happy and grateful now that....

____

____

____

____

____

____

____

____

____

Received on: ____________

"I have evidence of my abundance."

Step 1: Ask

Identify and be clear about what you want & desire.

Desired by : ____________

____

____

"I ask the universe for my desires."

Step 2: Allow

Expect that the Universe/God/Spirit will answer. Allow and be grateful AS IF you have already received what you want.

IT'S IMPORTANT TO FEEL GOOD ((((((**GOOD**))))))

Remember: thoughts = creation. If these thoughts are attached to powerful emotions (good or bad) that speeds up the creation of your desires.

VISUALIZE!!! *See it, feel it! This is where action begins*

Step 3: Receive

Be grateful and notice even the smallest evidence of the law of attraction. The more you are grateful and paying attention, the faster your desires and goals will manifests.

Start by using this sentence for all that you receive: "I'm so happy and grateful now that....

___

___

___

___

___

___

___

___

___

Received on: ___

"I have evidence of my abundance."

Step 1: Ask

Identify and be clear about what you want & desire.

Desired by : ___________

"I ask the universe for my desires."

Step 2: Allow

Expect that the Universe/God/Spirit will answer. Allow and be grateful AS IF you have already received what you want.

IT'S IMPORTANT TO FEEL GOOD ((((((**GOOD**))))))

Remember: thoughts = creation. If these thoughts are attached to powerful emotions (good or bad) that speeds up the creation of your desires.

VISUALIZE!!! *See it, feel it! This is where action begins*

Step 3: Receive

Be grateful and notice even the smallest evidence of the law of attraction. The more you are grateful and paying attention, the faster your desires and goals will manifests.

Start by using this sentence for all that you receive: "I'm so happy and grateful now that....

____

____

____

____

____

____

____

____

____

Received on: ______________

"I have evidence of my abundance."

Step 1: Ask

Identify and be clear about what you want & desire.

Desired by : ____________

"I ask the universe for my desires."

Step 2: Allow

Expect that the Universe/God/Spirit will answer. Allow and be grateful AS IF you have already received what you want.

IT'S IMPORTANT TO FEEL GOOD ((((((**GOOD**))))))

Remember: thoughts = creation. If these thoughts are attached to powerful emotions (good or bad) that speeds up the creation of your desires.

VISUALIZE!!! *See it, feel it! This is where action begins*

Step 3: Receive

Be grateful and notice even the smallest evidence of the law of attraction. The more you are grateful and paying attention, the faster your desires and goals will manifests.

Start by using this sentence for all that you receive: "I'm so happy and grateful now that....

____

____

____

____

____

____

____

____

____

Received on: ____________

"I have evidence of my abundance."

Step 1: Ask

Identify and be clear about what you want & desire.

Desired by : ____________

"I ask the universe for my desires."

Step 2: Allow

Expect that the Universe/God/Spirit will answer. Allow and be grateful AS IF you have already received what you want.

IT'S IMPORTANT TO FEEL GOOD ((((((**GOOD**))))))

Remember: thoughts = creation. If these thoughts are attached to powerful emotions (good or bad) that speeds up the creation of your desires.

VISUALIZE!!! *See it, feel it! This is where action begins*

Step 3: Receive

Be grateful and notice even the smallest evidence of the law of attraction. The more you are grateful and paying attention, the faster your desires and goals will manifests.

Start by using this sentence for all that you receive: "I'm so happy and grateful now that....

____

____

____

____

____

____

____

____

____

Received on: ______________

"I have evidence of my abundance."

Step 1: Ask

Identify and be clear about what you want & desire.

Desired by : ____________

"I ask the universe for my desires."

Step 2: Allow

Expect that the Universe/God/Spirit will answer. Allow and be grateful AS IF you have already received what you want.

IT'S IMPORTANT TO FEEL GOOD ((((((**GOOD**))))))

Remember: thoughts = creation. If these thoughts are attached to powerful emotions (good or bad) that speeds up the creation of your desires.

VISUALIZE!!! *See it, feel it! This is where action begins*

Step 3: Receive

Be grateful and notice even the smallest evidence of the law of attraction. The more you are grateful and paying attention, the faster your desires and goals will manifests.

Start by using this sentence for all that you receive: "I'm so happy and grateful now that....

____

____

____

____

____

____

____

____

____

Received on: ____________

"I have evidence of my abundance."

Step 1: Ask

Identify and be clear about what you want & desire.

Desired by : ____________

___

___

"I ask the universe for my desires."

Step 2: Allow

Expect that the Universe/God/Spirit will answer. Allow and be grateful AS IF you have already received what you want.

IT'S IMPORTANT TO FEEL GOOD ((((((**GOOD**))))))

Remember: thoughts = creation. If these thoughts are attached to powerful emotions (good or bad) that speeds up the creation of your desires.

VISUALIZE!!! *See it, feel it! This is where action begins*

Step 3: Receive

Be grateful and notice even the smallest evidence of the law of attraction. The more you are grateful and paying attention, the faster your desires and goals will manifests.

Start by using this sentence for all that you receive: "I'm so happy and grateful now that....

____

____

____

____

____

____

____

____

____

Received on: ____________

"I have evidence of my abundance."

Step 1: Ask

Identify and be clear about what you want & desire.

Desired by : ____________

____

____

"I ask the universe for my desires."

Step 2: Allow

Expect that the Universe/God/Spirit will answer. Allow and be grateful AS IF you have already received what you want.

IT'S IMPORTANT TO FEEL GOOD ((((((**GOOD**))))))

Remember: thoughts = creation. If these thoughts are attached to powerful emotions (good or bad) that speeds up the creation of your desires.

VISUALIZE!!! *See it, feel it! This is where action begins*

Step 3: Receive

Be grateful and notice even the smallest evidence of the law of attraction. The more you are grateful and paying attention, the faster your desires and goals will manifests.

Start by using this sentence for all that you receive: "I'm so happy and grateful now that....

___

___

___

___

___

___

___

___

___

Received on: ___________

"I have evidence of my abundance."

Step 1: Ask

Identify and be clear about what you want & desire.

Desired by: ____________

"I ask the universe for my desires."

Step 2: Allow

Expect that the Universe/God/Spirit will answer. Allow and be grateful AS IF you have already received what you want.

IT'S IMPORTANT TO FEEL GOOD ((((((**GOOD**))))))

Remember: thoughts = creation. If these thoughts are attached to powerful emotions (good or bad) that speeds up the creation of your desires.

VISUALIZE!!! *See it, feel it! This is where action begins*

Step 3: Receive

Be grateful and notice even the smallest evidence of the law of attraction. The more you are grateful and paying attention, the faster your desires and goals will manifests.

Start by using this sentence for all that you receive: "I'm so happy and grateful now that....

____

____

____

____

____

____

____

____

____

Received on: _______________

"I have evidence of my abundance."

Step 1: Ask

Identify and be clear about what you want & desire.

Desired by : ____________

"I ask the universe for my desires."

Step 2: Allow

Expect that the Universe/God/Spirit will answer. Allow and be grateful AS IF you have already received what you want.

IT'S IMPORTANT TO FEEL GOOD ((((((**GOOD**))))))

Remember: thoughts = creation. If these thoughts are attached to powerful emotions (good or bad) that speeds up the creation of your desires.

VISUALIZE!!! *See it, feel it! This is where action begins*

Step 3: Receive

Be grateful and notice even the smallest evidence of the law of attraction. The more you are grateful and paying attention, the faster your desires and goals will manifests.

Start by using this sentence for all that you receive: "I'm so happy and grateful now that....

____

____

____

____

____

____

____

____

____

Received on: ______________

"I have evidence of my abundance."

Step 1: Ask

Identify and be clear about what you want & desire.

Desired by : ____________

"I ask the universe for my desires."

Step 2: Allow

Expect that the Universe/God/Spirit will answer. Allow and be grateful AS IF you have already received what you want.

IT'S IMPORTANT TO FEEL GOOD ((((((**GOOD**))))))

Remember: thoughts = creation. If these thoughts are attached to powerful emotions (good or bad) that speeds up the creation of your desires.

VISUALIZE!!! *See it, feel it! This is where action begins*

Step 3: Receive

Be grateful and notice even the smallest evidence of the law of attraction. The more you are grateful and paying attention, the faster your desires and goals will manifests.

Start by using this sentence for all that you receive: "I'm so happy and grateful now that....

____

____

____

____

____

____

____

____

____

Received on: ____________

"I have evidence of my abundance."

Step 1: Ask

Identify and be clear about what you want & desire.

Desired by : ____________

"I ask the universe for my desires."

Step 2: Allow

Expect that the Universe/God/Spirit will answer. Allow and be grateful AS IF you have already received what you want.

IT'S IMPORTANT TO FEEL GOOD ((((((**GOOD**))))))

Remember: thoughts = creation. If these thoughts are attached to powerful emotions (good or bad) that speeds up the creation of your desires.

VISUALIZE!!! *See it, feel it! This is where action begins*

Step 3: Receive

Be grateful and notice even the smallest evidence of the law of attraction. The more you are grateful and paying attention, the faster your desires and goals will manifests.

Start by using this sentence for all that you receive: "I'm so happy and grateful now that....

____

____

____

____

____

____

____

____

____

Received on: ____________

"I have evidence of my abundance."

Step 1: Ask

Identify and be clear about what you want & desire.

Desired by : ____________

____

____

"I ask the universe for my desires."

Step 2: Allow

Expect that the Universe/God/Spirit will answer. Allow and be grateful AS IF you have already received what you want.

IT'S IMPORTANT TO FEEL GOOD ((((((**GOOD**))))))

Remember: thoughts = creation. If these thoughts are attached to powerful emotions (good or bad) that speeds up the creation of your desires.

VISUALIZE!!! *See it, feel it! This is where action begins*

Step 3: Receive

Be grateful and notice even the smallest evidence of the law of attraction. The more you are grateful and paying attention, the faster your desires and goals will manifests.

Start by using this sentence for all that you receive: "I'm so happy and grateful now that....

____

____

____

____

____

____

____

____

____

Received on: ______________

"I have evidence of my abundance."

Step 1: Ask

Identify and be clear about what you want & desire.

Desired by : ___________

"I ask the universe for my desires."

Step 2: Allow

Expect that the Universe/God/Spirit will answer. Allow and be grateful AS IF you have already received what you want.

IT'S IMPORTANT TO FEEL GOOD ((((((**GOOD**))))))

Remember: thoughts = creation. If these thoughts are attached to powerful emotions (good or bad) that speeds up the creation of your desires.

VISUALIZE!!! *See it, feel it! This is where action begins*

Step 3: Receive

Be grateful and notice even the smallest evidence of the law of attraction. The more you are grateful and paying attention, the faster your desires and goals will manifests.

Start by using this sentence for all that you receive: "I'm so happy and grateful now that....

____

____

____

____

____

____

____

____

____

Received on: ____________

"I have evidence of my abundance."

Step 1: Ask

Identify and be clear about what you want & desire.

Desired by : ____________

____

____

"I ask the universe for my desires."

Step 2: Allow

Expect that the Universe/God/Spirit will answer. Allow and be grateful AS IF you have already received what you want.

IT'S IMPORTANT TO FEEL GOOD ((((((**GOOD**))))))

Remember: thoughts = creation. If these thoughts are attached to powerful emotions (good or bad) that speeds up the creation of your desires.

VISUALIZE!!! *See it, feel it! This is where action begins*

Step 3: Receive

Be grateful and notice even the smallest evidence of the law of attraction. The more you are grateful and paying attention, the faster your desires and goals will manifests.

Start by using this sentence for all that you receive: "I'm so happy and grateful now that....

____

____

____

____

____

____

____

____

____

Received on: ________________

"I have evidence of my abundance."

Step 1: Ask

Identify and be clear about what you want & desire.

Desired by : ____________

____

____

"I ask the universe for my desires."

Step 2: Allow

Expect that the Universe/God/Spirit will answer. Allow and be grateful AS IF you have already received what you want.

IT'S IMPORTANT TO FEEL GOOD ((((((**GOOD**))))))

Remember: thoughts = creation. If these thoughts are attached to powerful emotions (good or bad) that speeds up the creation of your desires.

VISUALIZE!!! *See it, feel it! This is where action begins*

Step 3: Receive

Be grateful and notice even the smallest evidence of the law of attraction. The more you are grateful and paying attention, the faster your desires and goals will manifests.

Start by using this sentence for all that you receive: "I'm so happy and grateful now that....

____

____

____

____

____

____

____

____

____

Received on: ____________

"I have evidence of my abundance."

Step 1: Ask

Identify and be clear about what you want & desire.

Desired by : ____________

"I ask the universe for my desires."

Step 2: Allow

Expect that the Universe/God/Spirit will answer. Allow and be grateful AS IF you have already received what you want.

IT'S IMPORTANT TO FEEL GOOD ((((((**GOOD**))))))

Remember: thoughts = creation. If these thoughts are attached to powerful emotions (good or bad) that speeds up the creation of your desires.

VISUALIZE!!! *See it, feel it! This is where action begins*

Step 3: Receive

Be grateful and notice even the smallest evidence of the law of attraction. The more you are grateful and paying attention, the faster your desires and goals will manifests.

Start by using this sentence for all that you receive: "I'm so happy and grateful now that....

____

____

____

____

____

____

____

____

____

Received on: ______________

"I have evidence of my abundance."

Step 1: Ask

Identify and be clear about what you want & desire.

Desired by : ____________

"I ask the universe for my desires."

Step 2: Allow

Expect that the Universe/God/Spirit will answer. Allow and be grateful AS IF you have already received what you want.

IT'S IMPORTANT TO FEEL GOOD ((((((**GOOD**))))))

Remember: thoughts = creation. If these thoughts are attached to powerful emotions (good or bad) that speeds up the creation of your desires.

VISUALIZE!!! *See it, feel it! This is where action begins*

Step 3: Receive

Be grateful and notice even the smallest evidence of the law of attraction. The more you are grateful and paying attention, the faster your desires and goals will manifests.

Start by using this sentence for all that you receive: "I'm so happy and grateful now that....

____

____

____

____

____

____

____

____

____

Received on: ______________

"I have evidence of my abundance."

Step 1: Ask

Identify and be clear about what you want & desire.

Desired by : ____________

"*I ask the universe for my desires.*"

Step 2: Allow

Expect that the Universe/God/Spirit will answer. Allow and be grateful AS IF you have already received what you want.

IT'S IMPORTANT TO FEEL GOOD ((((((**GOOD**))))))

Remember: thoughts = creation. If these thoughts are attached to powerful emotions (good or bad) that speeds up the creation of your desires.

VISUALIZE!!! *See it, feel it! This is where action begins*

Step 3: Receive

Be grateful and notice even the smallest evidence of the law of attraction. The more you are grateful and paying attention, the faster your desires and goals will manifests.

Start by using this sentence for all that you receive: "I'm so happy and grateful now that....

____

____

____

____

____

____

____

____

____

Received on: ____________

"I have evidence of my abundance."

Step 1: Ask

Identify and be clear about what you want & desire.

Desired by: ____________

"I ask the universe for my desires."

Step 2: Allow

Expect that the Universe/God/Spirit will answer. Allow and be grateful AS IF you have already received what you want.

IT'S IMPORTANT TO FEEL GOOD ((((((**GOOD**))))))

Remember: thoughts = creation. If these thoughts are attached to powerful emotions (good or bad) that speeds up the creation of your desires.

VISUALIZE!!! *See it, feel it! This is where action begins*

Step 3: Receive

Be grateful and notice even the smallest evidence of the law of attraction. The more you are grateful and paying attention, the faster your desires and goals will manifests.

Start by using this sentence for all that you receive: "I'm so happy and grateful now that....

____

____

____

____

____

____

____

____

____

Received on: ________________

"I have evidence of my abundance."

Step 1: Ask

Identify and be clear about what you want & desire.

Desired by : ____________

"I ask the universe for my desires."

Step 2: Allow

Expect that the Universe/God/Spirit will answer. Allow and be grateful AS IF you have already received what you want.

IT'S IMPORTANT TO FEEL GOOD ((((((**GOOD**))))))

Remember: thoughts = creation. If these thoughts are attached to powerful emotions (good or bad) that speeds up the creation of your desires.

VISUALIZE!!! *See it, feel it! This is where action begins*

Step 3: Receive

Be grateful and notice even the smallest evidence of the law of attraction. The more you are grateful and paying attention, the faster your desires and goals will manifests.

Start by using this sentence for all that you receive: "I'm so happy and grateful now that....

____

Received on: _______________

"I have evidence of my abundance."

Step 1: Ask

Identify and be clear about what you want & desire.

Desired by: ____________

____

____

"I ask the universe for my desires."

Step 2: Allow

Expect that the Universe/God/Spirit will answer. Allow and be grateful AS IF you have already received what you want.

IT'S IMPORTANT TO FEEL GOOD ((((((**GOOD**))))))

Remember: thoughts = creation. If these thoughts are attached to powerful emotions (good or bad) that speeds up the creation of your desires.

VISUALIZE!!! *See it, feel it! This is where action begins*

Step 3: Receive

Be grateful and notice even the smallest evidence of the law of attraction. The more you are grateful and paying attention, the faster your desires and goals will manifests.

Start by using this sentence for all that you receive: "I'm so happy and grateful now that....

____

____

____

____

____

____

____

____

____

Received on: ______________

"I have evidence of my abundance."

Step 1: Ask

Identify and be clear about what you want & desire.

Desired by : ___________

"I ask the universe for my desires."

Step 2: Allow

Expect that the Universe/God/Spirit will answer. Allow and be grateful AS IF you have already received what you want.

IT'S IMPORTANT TO FEEL GOOD ((((((**GOOD**))))))

Remember: thoughts = creation. If these thoughts are attached to powerful emotions (good or bad) that speeds up the creation of your desires.

VISUALIZE!!! *See it, feel it! This is where action begins*

Step 3: Receive

Be grateful and notice even the smallest evidence of the law of attraction. The more you are grateful and paying attention, the faster your desires and goals will manifests.

Start by using this sentence for all that you receive: "I'm so happy and grateful now that....

____

____

____

____

____

____

____

____

____

Received on: ______________

"I have evidence of my abundance."

Step 1: Ask

Identify and be clear about what you want & desire.

Desired by : ____________

"I ask the universe for my desires."

Step 2: Allow

Expect that the Universe/God/Spirit will answer. Allow and be grateful AS IF you have already received what you want.

IT'S IMPORTANT TO FEEL GOOD ((((((**GOOD**))))))

Remember: thoughts = creation. If these thoughts are attached to powerful emotions (good or bad) that speeds up the creation of your desires.

VISUALIZE!!! *See it, feel it! This is where action begins*

Step 3: Receive

Be grateful and notice even the smallest evidence of the law of attraction. The more you are grateful and paying attention, the faster your desires and goals will manifests.

Start by using this sentence for all that you receive: "I'm so happy and grateful now that....

____

____

____

____

____

____

____

____

____

Received on: ______________

"I have evidence of my abundance."

Step 1: Ask

Identify and be clear about what you want & desire.

Desired by : ____________

"I ask the universe for my desires."

Step 2: Allow

Expect that the Universe/God/Spirit will answer. Allow and be grateful AS IF you have already received what you want.

IT'S IMPORTANT TO FEEL GOOD ((((((**GOOD**))))))

Remember: thoughts = creation. If these thoughts are attached to powerful emotions (good or bad) that speeds up the creation of your desires.

VISUALIZE!!! *See it, feel it! This is where action begins*

Step 3: Receive

Be grateful and notice even the smallest evidence of the law of attraction. The more you are grateful and paying attention, the faster your desires and goals will manifests.

Start by using this sentence for all that you receive: "I'm so happy and grateful now that....

____

____

____

____

____

____

____

____

____

Received on: ____________

"I have evidence of my abundance."

Step 1: Ask

Identify and be clear about what you want & desire.

Desired by : ____________

____

____

"I ask the universe for my desires."

Step 2: Allow

Expect that the Universe/God/Spirit will answer. Allow and be grateful AS IF you have already received what you want.

IT'S IMPORTANT TO FEEL GOOD ((((((**GOOD**))))))

Remember: thoughts = creation. If these thoughts are attached to powerful emotions (good or bad) that speeds up the creation of your desires.

VISUALIZE!!! *See it, feel it! This is where action begins*

Step 3: Receive

Be grateful and notice even the smallest evidence of the law of attraction. The more you are grateful and paying attention, the faster your desires and goals will manifests.

Start by using this sentence for all that you receive: "I'm so happy and grateful now that....

____

____

____

____

____

____

____

____

____

Received on: ____________

"I have evidence of my abundance."

Step 1: Ask

Identify and be clear about what you want & desire.

Desired by : ____________

____

____

"I ask the universe for my desires."

Step 2: Allow

Expect that the Universe/God/Spirit will answer. Allow and be grateful AS IF you have already received what you want.

IT'S IMPORTANT TO FEEL GOOD ((((((**GOOD**))))))

Remember: thoughts = creation. If these thoughts are attached to powerful emotions (good or bad) that speeds up the creation of your desires.

VISUALIZE!!! *See it, feel it! This is where action begins*

Step 3: Receive

Be grateful and notice even the smallest evidence of the law of attraction. The more you are grateful and paying attention, the faster your desires and goals will manifests.

Start by using this sentence for all that you receive: "I'm so happy and grateful now that....

___

___

___

___

___

___

___

___

___

Received on: ____________

"I have evidence of my abundance."

Step 1: Ask

Identify and be clear about what you want & desire.

Desired by : ____________

____

____

"I ask the universe for my desires."

Step 2: Allow

Expect that the Universe/God/Spirit will answer. Allow and be grateful AS IF you have already received what you want.

IT'S IMPORTANT TO FEEL GOOD ((((((**GOOD**))))))

Remember: thoughts = creation. If these thoughts are attached to powerful emotions (good or bad) that speeds up the creation of your desires.

VISUALIZE!!! *See it, feel it! This is where action begins*

Step 3: Receive

Be grateful and notice even the smallest evidence of the law of attraction. The more you are grateful and paying attention, the faster your desires and goals will manifests.

Start by using this sentence for all that you receive: "I'm so happy and grateful now that....

____

____

____

____

____

____

____

____

____

Received on: ____________

"I have evidence of my abundance."

Step 1: Ask

Identify and be clear about what you want & desire.

Desired by: ____________

____

____

"I ask the universe for my desires."

Step 2: Allow

Expect that the Universe/God/Spirit will answer. Allow and be grateful AS IF you have already received what you want.

IT'S IMPORTANT TO FEEL GOOD ((((((**GOOD**))))))

Remember: thoughts = creation. If these thoughts are attached to powerful emotions (good or bad) that speeds up the creation of your desires.

VISUALIZE!!! *See it, feel it! This is where action begins*

Step 3: Receive

Be grateful and notice even the smallest evidence of the law of attraction. The more you are grateful and paying attention, the faster your desires and goals will manifests.

Start by using this sentence for all that you receive: "I'm so happy and grateful now that....

____

____

____

____

____

____

____

____

____

Received on: ____________

"I have evidence of my abundance."

Step 1: Ask

Identify and be clear about what you want & desire.

Desired by : ____________

"I ask the universe for my desires."

Step 2: Allow

Expect that the Universe/God/Spirit will answer. Allow and be grateful AS IF you have already received what you want.

IT'S IMPORTANT TO FEEL GOOD ((((((**GOOD**))))))

Remember: thoughts = creation. If these thoughts are attached to powerful emotions (good or bad) that speeds up the creation of your desires.

VISUALIZE!!! *See it, feel it! This is where action begins*

Step 3: Receive

Be grateful and notice even the smallest evidence of the law of attraction. The more you are grateful and paying attention, the faster your desires and goals will manifests.

Start by using this sentence for all that you receive: "I'm so happy and grateful now that....

____

____

____

____

____

____

____

____

____

Received on: ______________

"I have evidence of my abundance."

Step 1: Ask

Identify and be clear about what you want & desire.

Desired by : ___________

____

____

"I ask the universe for my desires."

Step 2: Allow

Expect that the Universe/God/Spirit will answer. Allow and be grateful AS IF you have already received what you want.

IT'S IMPORTANT TO FEEL GOOD ((((((**GOOD**))))))

Remember: thoughts = creation. If these thoughts are attached to powerful emotions (good or bad) that speeds up the creation of your desires.

VISUALIZE!!! *See it, feel it! This is where action begins*

Step 3: Receive

Be grateful and notice even the smallest evidence of the law of attraction. The more you are grateful and paying attention, the faster your desires and goals will manifests.

Start by using this sentence for all that you receive: "I'm so happy and grateful now that....

____

____

____

____

____

____

____

____

____

Received on: ____________

"I have evidence of my abundance."

Step 1: Ask

Identify and be clear about what you want & desire.

Desired by : ____________

"I ask the universe for my desires."

Step 2: Allow

Expect that the Universe/God/Spirit will answer. Allow and be grateful AS IF you have already received what you want.

IT'S IMPORTANT TO FEEL GOOD ((((((**GOOD**))))))

Remember: thoughts = creation. If these thoughts are attached to powerful emotions (good or bad) that speeds up the creation of your desires.

VISUALIZE!!! *See it, feel it! This is where action begins*

Step 3: Receive

Be grateful and notice even the smallest evidence of the law of attraction. The more you are grateful and paying attention, the faster your desires and goals will manifests.

Start by using this sentence for all that you receive: "I'm so happy and grateful now that....

___

___

___

___

___

___

___

___

___

Received on: ___

"I have evidence of my abundance."

Step 1: Ask

Identify and be clear about what you want & desire.

Desired by : __________

"I ask the universe for my desires."

Step 2: Allow

Expect that the Universe/God/Spirit will answer. Allow and be grateful AS IF you have already received what you want.

IT'S IMPORTANT TO FEEL GOOD ((((((**GOOD**))))))

Remember: thoughts = creation. If these thoughts are attached to powerful emotions (good or bad) that speeds up the creation of your desires.

VISUALIZE!!! *See it, feel it! This is where action begins*

Step 3: Receive

Be grateful and notice even the smallest evidence of the law of attraction. The more you are grateful and paying attention, the faster your desires and goals will manifests.

Start by using this sentence for all that you receive: "I'm so happy and grateful now that....

____

____

____

____

____

____

____

____

____

Received on: ______________

"I have evidence of my abundance."

Step 1: Ask

Identify and be clear about what you want & desire.

Desired by : ______________

"I ask the universe for my desires."

Step 2: Allow

Expect that the Universe/God/Spirit will answer. Allow and be grateful AS IF you have already received what you want.

IT'S IMPORTANT TO FEEL GOOD ((((((**GOOD**))))))

Remember: thoughts = creation. If these thoughts are attached to powerful emotions (good or bad) that speeds up the creation of your desires.

VISUALIZE!!! *See it, feel it! This is where action begins*

Step 3: Receive

Be grateful and notice even the smallest evidence of the law of attraction. The more you are grateful and paying attention, the faster your desires and goals will manifests.

Start by using this sentence for all that you receive: "I'm so happy and grateful now that....

____

____

____

____

____

____

____

____

____

Received on: ______________

"I have evidence of my abundance."

Step 1: Ask

Identify and be clear about what you want & desire.

Desired by : ___________

"I ask the universe for my desires."

Step 2: Allow

Expect that the Universe/God/Spirit will answer. Allow and be grateful AS IF you have already received what you want.

IT'S IMPORTANT TO FEEL GOOD ((((((**GOOD**))))))

Remember: thoughts = creation. If these thoughts are attached to powerful emotions (good or bad) that speeds up the creation of your desires.

VISUALIZE!!! *See it, feel it! This is where action begins*

Step 3: Receive

Be grateful and notice even the smallest evidence of the law of attraction. The more you are grateful and paying attention, the faster your desires and goals will manifests.

Start by using this sentence for all that you receive: "I'm so happy and grateful now that....

____

____

____

____

____

____

____

____

____

Received on: ______________

"I have evidence of my abundance."

Step 1: Ask

Identify and be clear about what you want & desire.

Desired by : ____________

"I ask the universe for my desires."

Step 2: Allow

Expect that the Universe/God/Spirit will answer. Allow and be grateful AS IF you have already received what you want.

IT'S IMPORTANT TO FEEL GOOD ((((((**GOOD**))))))

Remember: thoughts = creation. If these thoughts are attached to powerful emotions (good or bad) that speeds up the creation of your desires.

VISUALIZE!!! *See it, feel it! This is where action begins*

Step 3: Receive

Be grateful and notice even the smallest evidence of the law of attraction. The more you are grateful and paying attention, the faster your desires and goals will manifests.

Start by using this sentence for all that you receive: "I'm so happy and grateful now that....

___

___

___

___

___

___

___

___

___

Received on: ______________

"I have evidence of my abundance."

Step 1: Ask

Identify and be clear about what you want & desire.

Desired by : ___________

____

____

"I ask the universe for my desires."

Step 2: Allow

Expect that the Universe/God/Spirit will answer. Allow and be grateful AS IF you have already received what you want.

IT'S IMPORTANT TO FEEL GOOD ((((((**GOOD**))))))

Remember: thoughts = creation. If these thoughts are attached to powerful emotions (good or bad) that speeds up the creation of your desires.

VISUALIZE!!! *See it, feel it! This is where action begins*

Step 3: Receive

Be grateful and notice even the smallest evidence of the law of attraction. The more you are grateful and paying attention, the faster your desires and goals will manifests.

Start by using this sentence for all that you receive: "I'm so happy and grateful now that....

___

___

___

___

___

___

___

___

___

Received on: ___

"I have evidence of my abundance."

Step 1: Ask

Identify and be clear about what you want & desire.

Desired by : ____________

___

___

"I ask the universe for my desires."

Step 2: Allow

Expect that the Universe/God/Spirit will answer. Allow and be grateful AS IF you have already received what you want.

IT'S IMPORTANT TO FEEL GOOD ((((((**GOOD**))))))

Remember: thoughts = creation. If these thoughts are attached to powerful emotions (good or bad) that speeds up the creation of your desires.

VISUALIZE!!! *See it, feel it! This is where action begins*

Step 3: Receive

Be grateful and notice even the smallest evidence of the law of attraction. The more you are grateful and paying attention, the faster your desires and goals will manifests.

Start by using this sentence for all that you receive: "I'm so happy and grateful now that....

Received on: ____________

"I have evidence of my abundance."

Step 1: Ask

Identify and be clear about what you want & desire.

Desired by : ___________

"I ask the universe for my desires."

Step 2: Allow

Expect that the Universe/God/Spirit will answer. Allow and be grateful AS IF you have already received what you want.

IT'S IMPORTANT TO FEEL GOOD ((((((**GOOD**))))))

Remember: thoughts = creation. If these thoughts are attached to powerful emotions (good or bad) that speeds up the creation of your desires.

VISUALIZE!!! *See it, feel it! This is where action begins*

Step 3: Receive

Be grateful and notice even the smallest evidence of the law of attraction. The more you are grateful and paying attention, the faster your desires and goals will manifests.

Start by using this sentence for all that you receive: "I'm so happy and grateful now that....

____

____

____

____

____

____

____

____

____

Received on: ____________

"I have evidence of my abundance."

Step 1: Ask

Identify and be clear about what you want & desire.

Desired by : ____________

"I ask the universe for my desires."

Step 2: Allow

Expect that the Universe/God/Spirit will answer. Allow and be grateful AS IF you have already received what you want.

IT'S IMPORTANT TO FEEL GOOD ((((((**GOOD**))))))

Remember: thoughts = creation. If these thoughts are attached to powerful emotions (good or bad) that speeds up the creation of your desires.

VISUALIZE!!! *See it, feel it! This is where action begins*

Step 3: Receive

Be grateful and notice even the smallest evidence of the law of attraction. The more you are grateful and paying attention, the faster your desires and goals will manifests.

Start by using this sentence for all that you receive: "I'm so happy and grateful now that....

Received on: __________

"I have evidence of my abundance."

Step 1: Ask

Identify and be clear about what you want & desire.

Desired by : ____________

____

____

"I ask the universe for my desires."

Step 2: Allow

Expect that the Universe/God/Spirit will answer. Allow and be grateful AS IF you have already received what you want.

IT'S IMPORTANT TO FEEL GOOD ((((((**GOOD**))))))

Remember: thoughts = creation. If these thoughts are attached to powerful emotions (good or bad) that speeds up the creation of your desires.

VISUALIZE!!! *See it, feel it! This is where action begins*

Step 3: Receive

Be grateful and notice even the smallest evidence of the law of attraction. The more you are grateful and paying attention, the faster your desires and goals will manifests.

Start by using this sentence for all that you receive: "I'm so happy and grateful now that....

____

____

____

____

____

____

____

____

____

Received on: ______________

"I have evidence of my abundance."

Step 1: Ask

Identify and be clear about what you want & desire.

Desired by : ____________

____

____

"I ask the universe for my desires."

Step 2: Allow

Expect that the Universe/God/Spirit will answer. Allow and be grateful AS IF you have already received what you want.

IT'S IMPORTANT TO FEEL GOOD ((((((**GOOD**))))))

Remember: thoughts = creation. If these thoughts are attached to powerful emotions (good or bad) that speeds up the creation of your desires.

VISUALIZE!!! *See it, feel it! This is where action begins*

Step 3: Receive

Be grateful and notice even the smallest evidence of the law of attraction. The more you are grateful and paying attention, the faster your desires and goals will manifests.

Start by using this sentence for all that you receive: "I'm so happy and grateful now that....

____

____

____

____

____

____

____

____

____

Received on: ______________

"I have evidence of my abundance."

Step 1: Ask

Identify and be clear about what you want & desire.

Desired by : ____________

"I ask the universe for my desires."

Step 2: Allow

Expect that the Universe/God/Spirit will answer. Allow and be grateful AS IF you have already received what you want.

IT'S IMPORTANT TO FEEL GOOD ((((((**GOOD**))))))

Remember: thoughts = creation. If these thoughts are attached to powerful emotions (good or bad) that speeds up the creation of your desires.

VISUALIZE!!! *See it, feel it! This is where action begins*

Step 3: Receive

Be grateful and notice even the smallest evidence of the law of attraction. The more you are grateful and paying attention, the faster your desires and goals will manifests.

Start by using this sentence for all that you receive: "I'm so happy and grateful now that....

____

____

____

____

____

____

____

____

____

Received on: ____________

"I have evidence of my abundance."

Step 1: Ask

Identify and be clear about what you want & desire.

Desired by : ____________

____

____

"I ask the universe for my desires."

Step 2: Allow

Expect that the Universe/God/Spirit will answer. Allow and be grateful AS IF you have already received what you want.

IT'S IMPORTANT TO FEEL GOOD ((((((**GOOD**))))))

Remember: thoughts = creation. If these thoughts are attached to powerful emotions (good or bad) that speeds up the creation of your desires.

VISUALIZE!!! *See it, feel it! This is where action begins*

Step 3: Receive

Be grateful and notice even the smallest evidence of the law of attraction. The more you are grateful and paying attention, the faster your desires and goals will manifests.

Start by using this sentence for all that you receive: "I'm so happy and grateful now that....

____

____

____

____

____

____

____

____

____

Received on: ______________

"I have evidence of my abundance."

Step 1: Ask

Identify and be clear about what you want & desire.

Desired by : ___________

"I ask the universe for my desires."

Step 2: Allow

Expect that the Universe/God/Spirit will answer. Allow and be grateful AS IF you have already received what you want.

IT'S IMPORTANT TO FEEL GOOD ((((((**GOOD**))))))

Remember: thoughts = creation. If these thoughts are attached to powerful emotions (good or bad) that speeds up the creation of your desires.

VISUALIZE!!! *See it, feel it! This is where action begins*

Step 3: Receive

Be grateful and notice even the smallest evidence of the law of attraction. The more you are grateful and paying attention, the faster your desires and goals will manifests.

Start by using this sentence for all that you receive: "I'm so happy and grateful now that....

____

____

____

____

____

____

____

____

____

Received on: ____________

"I have evidence of my abundance."

Step 1: Ask

Identify and be clear about what you want & desire.

Desired by : ____________

"I ask the universe for my desires."

Step 2: Allow

Expect that the Universe/God/Spirit will answer. Allow and be grateful AS IF you have already received what you want.

IT'S IMPORTANT TO FEEL GOOD ((((((**GOOD**))))))

Remember: thoughts = creation. If these thoughts are attached to powerful emotions (good or bad) that speeds up the creation of your desires.

VISUALIZE!!! *See it, feel it! This is where action begins*

Step 3: Receive

Be grateful and notice even the smallest evidence of the law of attraction. The more you are grateful and paying attention, the faster your desires and goals will manifests.

Start by using this sentence for all that you receive: "I'm so happy and grateful now that....

____

____

____

____

____

____

____

____

____

Received on: ______________

"I have evidence of my abundance."

Step 1: Ask

Identify and be clear about what you want & desire.

Desired by: ____________

____

____

"I ask the universe for my desires."

Step 2: Allow

Expect that the Universe/God/Spirit will answer. Allow and be grateful AS IF you have already received what you want.

IT'S IMPORTANT TO FEEL GOOD ((((((**GOOD**))))))

Remember: thoughts = creation. If these thoughts are attached to powerful emotions (good or bad) that speeds up the creation of your desires.

VISUALIZE!!! *See it, feel it! This is where action begins*

Step 3: Receive

Be grateful and notice even the smallest evidence of the law of attraction. The more you are grateful and paying attention, the faster your desires and goals will manifests.

Start by using this sentence for all that you receive: "I'm so happy and grateful now that....

____

____

____

____

____

____

____

____

____

Received on: ______________

"I have evidence of my abundance."

Step 1: Ask

Identify and be clear about what you want & desire.

Desired by : ____________

"I ask the universe for my desires."

Step 2: Allow

Expect that the Universe/God/Spirit will answer. Allow and be grateful AS IF you have already received what you want.

IT'S IMPORTANT TO FEEL GOOD ((((((**GOOD**))))))

Remember: thoughts = creation. If these thoughts are attached to powerful emotions (good or bad) that speeds up the creation of your desires.

VISUALIZE!!! *See it, feel it! This is where action begins*

Step 3: Receive

Be grateful and notice even the smallest evidence of the law of attraction. The more you are grateful and paying attention, the faster your desires and goals will manifests.

Start by using this sentence for all that you receive: "I'm so happy and grateful now that....

___

___

___

___

___

___

___

___

___

Received on: ___

"I have evidence of my abundance."

Step 1: Ask

Identify and be clear about what you want & desire.

Desired by : ___________

___

___

"I ask the universe for my desires."

Step 2: Allow

Expect that the Universe/God/Spirit will answer. Allow and be grateful AS IF you have already received what you want.

IT'S IMPORTANT TO FEEL GOOD ((((((**GOOD**))))))

Remember: thoughts = creation. If these thoughts are attached to powerful emotions (good or bad) that speeds up the creation of your desires.

VISUALIZE!!! *See it, feel it! This is where action begins*

Step 3: Receive

Be grateful and notice even the smallest evidence of the law of attraction. The more you are grateful and paying attention, the faster your desires and goals will manifests.

Start by using this sentence for all that you receive: "I'm so happy and grateful now that....

____

____

____

____

____

____

____

____

____

Received on: ______________

"I have evidence of my abundance."

Step 1: Ask

Identify and be clear about what you want & desire.

Desired by : ___________

___

___

"I ask the universe for my desires."

Step 2: Allow

Expect that the Universe/God/Spirit will answer. Allow and be grateful AS IF you have already received what you want.

IT'S IMPORTANT TO FEEL GOOD ((((((**GOOD**))))))

Remember: thoughts = creation. If these thoughts are attached to powerful emotions (good or bad) that speeds up the creation of your desires.

VISUALIZE!!! *See it, feel it! This is where action begins*

Step 3: Receive

Be grateful and notice even the smallest evidence of the law of attraction. The more you are grateful and paying attention, the faster your desires and goals will manifests.

Start by using this sentence for all that you receive: "I'm so happy and grateful now that....

____

____

____

____

____

____

____

____

____

Received on: ____________

"I have evidence of my abundance."

Step 1: Ask

Identify and be clear about what you want & desire.

Desired by : ____________

"I ask the universe for my desires."

Step 2: Allow

Expect that the Universe/God/Spirit will answer. Allow and be grateful AS IF you have already received what you want.

IT'S IMPORTANT TO FEEL GOOD ((((((**GOOD**))))))

Remember: thoughts = creation. If these thoughts are attached to powerful emotions (good or bad) that speeds up the creation of your desires.

VISUALIZE!!! *See it, feel it! This is where action begins*

Step 3: Receive

Be grateful and notice even the smallest evidence of the law of attraction. The more you are grateful and paying attention, the faster your desires and goals will manifests.

Start by using this sentence for all that you receive: "I'm so happy and grateful now that....

____

____

____

____

____

____

____

____

____

Received on: ____________

"I have evidence of my abundance."

Step 1: Ask

Identify and be clear about what you want & desire.

Desired by : ___________

"I ask the universe for my desires."

Step 2: Allow

Expect that the Universe/God/Spirit will answer. Allow and be grateful AS IF you have already received what you want.

IT'S IMPORTANT TO FEEL GOOD ((((((**GOOD**))))))

Remember: thoughts = creation. If these thoughts are attached to powerful emotions (good or bad) that speeds up the creation of your desires.

VISUALIZE!!! *See it, feel it! This is where action begins*

Step 3: Receive

Be grateful and notice even the smallest evidence of the law of attraction. The more you are grateful and paying attention, the faster your desires and goals will manifests.

Start by using this sentence for all that you receive: "I'm so happy and grateful now that....

____

____

____

____

____

____

____

____

____

Received on: ______________

"I have evidence of my abundance."

Step 1: Ask

Identify and be clear about what you want & desire.

Desired by : ____________

"I ask the universe for my desires."

Step 2: Allow

Expect that the Universe/God/Spirit will answer. Allow and be grateful AS IF you have already received what you want.

IT'S IMPORTANT TO FEEL GOOD ((((((**GOOD**))))))

Remember: thoughts = creation. If these thoughts are attached to powerful emotions (good or bad) that speeds up the creation of your desires.

VISUALIZE!!! *See it, feel it! This is where action begins*

Step 3: Receive

Be grateful and notice even the smallest evidence of the law of attraction. The more you are grateful and paying attention, the faster your desires and goals will manifests.

Start by using this sentence for all that you receive: "I'm so happy and grateful now that....

___

___

___

___

___

___

___

___

___

Received on: ___

"I have evidence of my abundance."

Step 1: Ask

Identify and be clear about what you want & desire.

Desired by : ____________

"I ask the universe for my desires."

Step 2: Allow

Expect that the Universe/God/Spirit will answer. Allow and be grateful AS IF you have already received what you want.

IT'S IMPORTANT TO FEEL GOOD ((((((**GOOD**))))))

Remember: thoughts = creation. If these thoughts are attached to powerful emotions (good or bad) that speeds up the creation of your desires.

VISUALIZE!!! *See it, feel it! This is where action begins*

Step 3: Receive

Be grateful and notice even the smallest evidence of the law of attraction. The more you are grateful and paying attention, the faster your desires and goals will manifests.

Start by using this sentence for all that you receive: "I'm so happy and grateful now that....

____

____

____

____

____

____

____

____

____

Received on: _______________

"I have evidence of my abundance."

Step 1: Ask

Identify and be clear about what you want & desire.

Desired by : ___________

"I ask the universe for my desires."

Step 2: Allow

Expect that the Universe/God/Spirit will answer. Allow and be grateful AS IF you have already received what you want.

IT'S IMPORTANT TO FEEL GOOD ((((((**GOOD**))))))

Remember: thoughts = creation. If these thoughts are attached to powerful emotions (good or bad) that speeds up the creation of your desires.

VISUALIZE!!! *See it, feel it! This is where action begins*

Step 3: Receive

Be grateful and notice even the smallest evidence of the law of attraction. The more you are grateful and paying attention, the faster your desires and goals will manifests.

Start by using this sentence for all that you receive: "I'm so happy and grateful now that....

Received on: ______________

"I have evidence of my abundance."

Step 1: Ask

Identify and be clear about what you want & desire.

Desired by : ____________

___

___

"I ask the universe for my desires."

Step 2: Allow

Expect that the Universe/God/Spirit will answer. Allow and be grateful AS IF you have already received what you want.

IT'S IMPORTANT TO FEEL GOOD ((((((**GOOD**))))))

Remember: thoughts = creation. If these thoughts are attached to powerful emotions (good or bad) that speeds up the creation of your desires.

VISUALIZE!!! *See it, feel it! This is where action begins*

Step 3: Receive

Be grateful and notice even the smallest evidence of the law of attraction. The more you are grateful and paying attention, the faster your desires and goals will manifests.

Start by using this sentence for all that you receive: "I'm so happy and grateful now that....

___

___

___

___

___

___

___

___

___

Received on: ________

"I have evidence of my abundance."

Step 1: Ask

Identify and be clear about what you want & desire.

Desired by : ____________

"I ask the universe for my desires."

Step 2: Allow

Expect that the Universe/God/Spirit will answer. Allow and be grateful AS IF you have already received what you want.

IT'S IMPORTANT TO FEEL GOOD ((((((**GOOD**))))))

Remember: thoughts = creation. If these thoughts are attached to powerful emotions (good or bad) that speeds up the creation of your desires.

VISUALIZE!!! *See it, feel it! This is where action begins*

Step 3: Receive

Be grateful and notice even the smallest evidence of the law of attraction. The more you are grateful and paying attention, the faster your desires and goals will manifests.

Start by using this sentence for all that you receive: "I'm so happy and grateful now that....

____

____

____

____

____

____

____

____

____

Received on: ____________

"I have evidence of my abundance."

Step 1: Ask

Identify and be clear about what you want & desire.

Desired by : ____________

"I ask the universe for my desires."

Step 2: Allow

Expect that the Universe/God/Spirit will answer. Allow and be grateful AS IF you have already received what you want.

IT'S IMPORTANT TO FEEL GOOD ((((((**GOOD**))))))

Remember: thoughts = creation. If these thoughts are attached to powerful emotions (good or bad) that speeds up the creation of your desires.

VISUALIZE!!! *See it, feel it! This is where action begins*

Step 3: Receive

Be grateful and notice even the smallest evidence of the law of attraction. The more you are grateful and paying attention, the faster your desires and goals will manifests.

Start by using this sentence for all that you receive: "I'm so happy and grateful now that....

____

____

____

____

____

____

____

____

____

Received on: ______________

"I have evidence of my abundance."

Step 1: Ask

Identify and be clear about what you want & desire.

Desired by : ___________

___

___

"I ask the universe for my desires."

Step 2: Allow

Expect that the Universe/God/Spirit will answer. Allow and be grateful AS IF you have already received what you want.

IT'S IMPORTANT TO FEEL GOOD ((((((**GOOD**))))))

Remember: thoughts = creation. If these thoughts are attached to powerful emotions (good or bad) that speeds up the creation of your desires.

VISUALIZE!!! *See it, feel it! This is where action begins*

Step 3: Receive

Be grateful and notice even the smallest evidence of the law of attraction. The more you are grateful and paying attention, the faster your desires and goals will manifests.

Start by using this sentence for all that you receive: "I'm so happy and grateful now that....

____

____

____

____

____

____

____

____

____

Received on: ____________

"I have evidence of my abundance."

Step 1: Ask

Identify and be clear about what you want & desire.

Desired by : ___________

"I ask the universe for my desires."

Step 2: Allow

Expect that the Universe/God/Spirit will answer. Allow and be grateful AS IF you have already received what you want.

IT'S IMPORTANT TO FEEL GOOD ((((((**GOOD**))))))

Remember: thoughts = creation. If these thoughts are attached to powerful emotions (good or bad) that speeds up the creation of your desires.

VISUALIZE!!! *See it, feel it! This is where action begins*

Step 3: Receive

Be grateful and notice even the smallest evidence of the law of attraction. The more you are grateful and paying attention, the faster your desires and goals will manifests.

Start by using this sentence for all that you receive: "I'm so happy and grateful now that....

____

____

____

____

____

____

____

____

____

Received on: ______________

"I have evidence of my abundance."

Step 1: Ask

Identify and be clear about what you want & desire.

Desired by : ____________

"I ask the universe for my desires."

Step 2: Allow

Expect that the Universe/God/Spirit will answer. Allow and be grateful AS IF you have already received what you want.

IT'S IMPORTANT TO FEEL GOOD ((((((**GOOD**))))))

Remember: thoughts = creation. If these thoughts are attached to powerful emotions (good or bad) that speeds up the creation of your desires.

VISUALIZE!!! *See it, feel it! This is where action begins*

Step 3: Receive

Be grateful and notice even the smallest evidence of the law of attraction. The more you are grateful and paying attention, the faster your desires and goals will manifests.

Start by using this sentence for all that you receive: "I'm so happy and grateful now that....

___

___

___

___

___

___

___

___

___

Received on: ___

"I have evidence of my abundance."

Step 1: Ask

Identify and be clear about what you want & desire.

Desired by : ____________

"I ask the universe for my desires."

Step 2: Allow

Expect that the Universe/God/Spirit will answer. Allow and be grateful AS IF you have already received what you want.

IT'S IMPORTANT TO FEEL GOOD ((((((**GOOD**))))))

Remember: thoughts = creation. If these thoughts are attached to powerful emotions (good or bad) that speeds up the creation of your desires.

VISUALIZE!!! *See it, feel it! This is where action begins*

Step 3: Receive

Be grateful and notice even the smallest evidence of the law of attraction. The more you are grateful and paying attention, the faster your desires and goals will manifests.

Start by using this sentence for all that you receive: "I'm so happy and grateful now that....

Received on: ____________

"I have evidence of my abundance."

Step 1: Ask

Identify and be clear about what you want & desire.

Desired by : ____________

____

____

"I ask the universe for my desires."

Step 2: Allow

Expect that the Universe/God/Spirit will answer. Allow and be grateful AS IF you have already received what you want.

IT'S IMPORTANT TO FEEL GOOD ((((((**GOOD**))))))

Remember: thoughts = creation. If these thoughts are attached to powerful emotions (good or bad) that speeds up the creation of your desires.

VISUALIZE!!! *See it, feel it! This is where action begins*

Step 3: Receive

Be grateful and notice even the smallest evidence of the law of attraction. The more you are grateful and paying attention, the faster your desires and goals will manifests.

Start by using this sentence for all that you receive: "I'm so happy and grateful now that....

____

____

____

____

____

____

____

____

____

Received on: ______________

"I have evidence of my abundance."

Step 1: Ask

Identify and be clear about what you want & desire.

Desired by : ____________

"I ask the universe for my desires."

Step 2: Allow

Expect that the Universe/God/Spirit will answer. Allow and be grateful AS IF you have already received what you want.

IT'S IMPORTANT TO FEEL GOOD ((((((**GOOD**))))))

Remember: thoughts = creation. If these thoughts are attached to powerful emotions (good or bad) that speeds up the creation of your desires.

VISUALIZE!!! *See it, feel it! This is where action begins*

Step 3: Receive

Be grateful and notice even the smallest evidence of the law of attraction. The more you are grateful and paying attention, the faster your desires and goals will manifests.

Start by using this sentence for all that you receive: "I'm so happy and grateful now that....

____

____

____

____

____

____

____

____

____

Received on: ____________

"I have evidence of my abundance."

Step 1: Ask

Identify and be clear about what you want & desire.

Desired by: ______________

____

____

"I ask the universe for my desires."

Step 2: Allow

Expect that the Universe/God/Spirit will answer. Allow and be grateful AS IF you have already received what you want.

IT'S IMPORTANT TO FEEL GOOD ((((((**GOOD**))))))

Remember: thoughts = creation. If these thoughts are attached to powerful emotions (good or bad) that speeds up the creation of your desires.

VISUALIZE!!! *See it, feel it! This is where action begins*

Step 3: Receive

Be grateful and notice even the smallest evidence of the law of attraction. The more you are grateful and paying attention, the faster your desires and goals will manifests.

Start by using this sentence for all that you receive: "I'm so happy and grateful now that....

Received on: ______________

"I have evidence of my abundance."

Step 1: Ask

Identify and be clear about what you want & desire.

Desired by : ____________

____

____

"I ask the universe for my desires."

Step 2: Allow

Expect that the Universe/God/Spirit will answer. Allow and be grateful AS IF you have already received what you want.

IT'S IMPORTANT TO FEEL GOOD ((((((**GOOD**))))))

Remember: thoughts = creation. If these thoughts are attached to powerful emotions (good or bad) that speeds up the creation of your desires.

VISUALIZE!!! *See it, feel it! This is where action begins*

Step 3: Receive

Be grateful and notice even the smallest evidence of the law of attraction. The more you are grateful and paying attention, the faster your desires and goals will manifests.

Start by using this sentence for all that you receive: "I'm so happy and grateful now that....

____

____

____

____

____

____

____

____

____

Received on: ______________

"I have evidence of my abundance."

Step 1: Ask

Identify and be clear about what you want & desire.

Desired by : ____________

____

____

"I ask the universe for my desires."

Step 2: Allow

Expect that the Universe/God/Spirit will answer. Allow and be grateful AS IF you have already received what you want.

IT'S IMPORTANT TO FEEL GOOD ((((((**GOOD**))))))

Remember: thoughts = creation. If these thoughts are attached to powerful emotions (good or bad) that speeds up the creation of your desires.

VISUALIZE!!! *See it, feel it! This is where action begins*

Step 3: Receive

Be grateful and notice even the smallest evidence of the law of attraction. The more you are grateful and paying attention, the faster your desires and goals will manifests.

Start by using this sentence for all that you receive: "I'm so happy and grateful now that....

____

____

____

____

____

____

____

____

____

Received on: ______________

"I have evidence of my abundance."

Step 1: Ask

Identify and be clear about what you want & desire.

Desired by : ____________

____

____

"I ask the universe for my desires."

Step 2: Allow

Expect that the Universe/God/Spirit will answer. Allow and be grateful AS IF you have already received what you want.

IT'S IMPORTANT TO FEEL GOOD ((((((**GOOD**))))))

Remember: thoughts = creation. If these thoughts are attached to powerful emotions (good or bad) that speeds up the creation of your desires.

VISUALIZE!!! *See it, feel it! This is where action begins*

Step 3: Receive

Be grateful and notice even the smallest evidence of the law of attraction. The more you are grateful and paying attention, the faster your desires and goals will manifests.

Start by using this sentence for all that you receive: "I'm so happy and grateful now that....

____

____

____

____

____

____

____

____

____

Received on: ______________

"I have evidence of my abundance."

Step 1: Ask

Identify and be clear about what you want & desire.

Desired by : ____________

"I ask the universe for my desires."

Step 2: Allow

Expect that the Universe/God/Spirit will answer. Allow and be grateful AS IF you have already received what you want.

IT'S IMPORTANT TO FEEL GOOD ((((((**GOOD**))))))

Remember: thoughts = creation. If these thoughts are attached to powerful emotions (good or bad) that speeds up the creation of your desires.

VISUALIZE!!! *See it, feel it! This is where action begins*

Step 3: Receive

Be grateful and notice even the smallest evidence of the law of attraction. The more you are grateful and paying attention, the faster your desires and goals will manifests.

Start by using this sentence for all that you receive: "I'm so happy and grateful now that....

____

____

____

____

____

____

____

____

____

Received on: ______________

"I have evidence of my abundance."

Step 1: Ask

Identify and be clear about what you want & desire.

Desired by : ____________

____

____

"I ask the universe for my desires."

Step 2: Allow

Expect that the Universe/God/Spirit will answer. Allow and be grateful AS IF you have already received what you want.

IT'S IMPORTANT TO FEEL GOOD ((((((**GOOD**))))))

Remember: thoughts = creation. If these thoughts are attached to powerful emotions (good or bad) that speeds up the creation of your desires.

VISUALIZE!!! *See it, feel it! This is where action begins*

Step 3: Receive

Be grateful and notice even the smallest evidence of the law of attraction. The more you are grateful and paying attention, the faster your desires and goals will manifests.

Start by using this sentence for all that you receive: "I'm so happy and grateful now that....

____

____

____

____

____

____

____

____

____

Received on: ______________

"I have evidence of my abundance."

Step 1: Ask

Identify and be clear about what you want & desire.

Desired by : ____________

"I ask the universe for my desires."

Step 2: Allow

Expect that the Universe/God/Spirit will answer. Allow and be grateful AS IF you have already received what you want.

IT'S IMPORTANT TO FEEL GOOD ((((((**GOOD**))))))

Remember: thoughts = creation. If these thoughts are attached to powerful emotions (good or bad) that speeds up the creation of your desires.

VISUALIZE!!! *See it, feel it! This is where action begins*

Step 3: Receive

Be grateful and notice even the smallest evidence of the law of attraction. The more you are grateful and paying attention, the faster your desires and goals will manifests.

Start by using this sentence for all that you receive: "I'm so happy and grateful now that....

____

____

____

____

____

____

____

____

____

Received on: ____________

"I have evidence of my abundance."

Step 1: Ask

Identify and be clear about what you want & desire.

Desired by : ____________

"I ask the universe for my desires."

Step 2: Allow

Expect that the Universe/God/Spirit will answer. Allow and be grateful AS IF you have already received what you want.

IT'S IMPORTANT TO FEEL GOOD ((((((**GOOD**))))))

Remember: thoughts = creation. If these thoughts are attached to powerful emotions (good or bad) that speeds up the creation of your desires.

VISUALIZE!!! *See it, feel it! This is where action begins*

Step 3: Receive

Be grateful and notice even the smallest evidence of the law of attraction. The more you are grateful and paying attention, the faster your desires and goals will manifests.

Start by using this sentence for all that you receive: "I'm so happy and grateful now that....

____

____

____

____

____

____

____

____

____

Received on: ______________

"I have evidence of my abundance."

Step 1: Ask

Identify and be clear about what you want & desire.

Desired by : ____________

"I ask the universe for my desires."

Step 2: Allow

Expect that the Universe/God/Spirit will answer. Allow and be grateful AS IF you have already received what you want.

IT'S IMPORTANT TO FEEL GOOD ((((((**GOOD**))))))

Remember: thoughts = creation. If these thoughts are attached to powerful emotions (good or bad) that speeds up the creation of your desires.

VISUALIZE!!! *See it, feel it! This is where action begins*

Step 3: Receive

Be grateful and notice even the smallest evidence of the law of attraction. The more you are grateful and paying attention, the faster your desires and goals will manifests.

Start by using this sentence for all that you receive: "I'm so happy and grateful now that....

___

___

___

___

___

___

___

___

___

Received on: ______________

"I have evidence of my abundance."

Step 1: Ask

Identify and be clear about what you want & desire.

Desired by : ___________

"I ask the universe for my desires."

Step 2: Allow

Expect that the Universe/God/Spirit will answer. Allow and be grateful AS IF you have already received what you want.

IT'S IMPORTANT TO FEEL GOOD ((((((**GOOD**))))))

Remember: thoughts = creation. If these thoughts are attached to powerful emotions (good or bad) that speeds up the creation of your desires.

VISUALIZE!!! *See it, feel it! This is where action begins*

Step 3: Receive

Be grateful and notice even the smallest evidence of the law of attraction. The more you are grateful and paying attention, the faster your desires and goals will manifests.

Start by using this sentence for all that you receive: "I'm so happy and grateful now that....

____

____

____

____

____

____

____

____

____

Received on: ______________

"I have evidence of my abundance."

Step 1: Ask

Identify and be clear about what you want & desire.

Desired by : ____________

"I ask the universe for my desires."

Step 2: Allow

Expect that the Universe/God/Spirit will answer. Allow and be grateful AS IF you have already received what you want.

IT'S IMPORTANT TO FEEL GOOD ((((((**GOOD**))))))

Remember: thoughts = creation. If these thoughts are attached to powerful emotions (good or bad) that speeds up the creation of your desires.

VISUALIZE!!! *See it, feel it! This is where action begins*

Step 3: Receive

Be grateful and notice even the smallest evidence of the law of attraction. The more you are grateful and paying attention, the faster your desires and goals will manifests.

Start by using this sentence for all that you receive: "I'm so happy and grateful now that....

____

____

____

____

____

____

____

____

____

Received on: ____________

"I have evidence of my abundance."

Step 1: Ask

Identify and be clear about what you want & desire.

Desired by : ____________

"I ask the universe for my desires."

Step 2: Allow

Expect that the Universe/God/Spirit will answer. Allow and be grateful AS IF you have already received what you want.

IT'S IMPORTANT TO FEEL GOOD ((((((**GOOD**))))))

Remember: thoughts = creation. If these thoughts are attached to powerful emotions (good or bad) that speeds up the creation of your desires.

VISUALIZE!!! *See it, feel it! This is where action begins*

Step 3: Receive

Be grateful and notice even the smallest evidence of the law of attraction. The more you are grateful and paying attention, the faster your desires and goals will manifests.

Start by using this sentence for all that you receive: "I'm so happy and grateful now that....

____

____

____

____

____

____

____

____

____

Received on: ____________

"I have evidence of my abundance."

Step 1: Ask

Identify and be clear about what you want & desire.

Desired by: ____________

____

____

"I ask the universe for my desires."

Step 2: Allow

Expect that the Universe/God/Spirit will answer. Allow and be grateful AS IF you have already received what you want.

IT'S IMPORTANT TO FEEL GOOD ((((((**GOOD**))))))

Remember: thoughts = creation. If these thoughts are attached to powerful emotions (good or bad) that speeds up the creation of your desires.

VISUALIZE!!! *See it, feel it! This is where action begins*

Step 3: Receive

Be grateful and notice even the smallest evidence of the law of attraction. The more you are grateful and paying attention, the faster your desires and goals will manifests.

Start by using this sentence for all that you receive: "I'm so happy and grateful now that....

____

____

____

____

____

____

____

____

____

Received on: ______________

"I have evidence of my abundance."

Step 1: Ask

Identify and be clear about what you want & desire.

Desired by : ____________

"I ask the universe for my desires."

Step 2: Allow

Expect that the Universe/God/Spirit will answer. Allow and be grateful AS IF you have already received what you want.

IT'S IMPORTANT TO FEEL GOOD ((((((**GOOD**))))))

Remember: thoughts = creation. If these thoughts are attached to powerful emotions (good or bad) that speeds up the creation of your desires.

VISUALIZE!!! *See it, feel it! This is where action begins*

Step 3: Receive

Be grateful and notice even the smallest evidence of the law of attraction. The more you are grateful and paying attention, the faster your desires and goals will manifests.

Start by using this sentence for all that you receive: "I'm so happy and grateful now that....

____

____

____

____

____

____

____

____

____

Received on: ____________

"I have evidence of my abundance."

Step 1: Ask

Identify and be clear about what you want & desire.

Desired by: ___________

____

____

"I ask the universe for my desires."

Step 2: Allow

Expect that the Universe/God/Spirit will answer. Allow and be grateful AS IF you have already received what you want.

IT'S IMPORTANT TO FEEL GOOD ((((((**GOOD**))))))

Remember: thoughts = creation. If these thoughts are attached to powerful emotions (good or bad) that speeds up the creation of your desires.

VISUALIZE!!! *See it, feel it! This is where action begins*

Step 3: Receive

Be grateful and notice even the smallest evidence of the law of attraction. The more you are grateful and paying attention, the faster your desires and goals will manifests.

Start by using this sentence for all that you receive: "I'm so happy and grateful now that....

Received on: ____________

"I have evidence of my abundance."

CPSIA information can be obtained at www.ICGtesting.com
Printed in the USA
LVOW10s1327130416

483449LV00021B/396/P

VIVIAN TENORIO